Data base Mesh

A large-Scale delivery of value driven by data

Epris E. Ezekiel

Contents

Introduction

An innovative method for managing analytical data called "data mesh" is based on a contemporary, networked architecture. It enables data to be easily accessed and queried by end users without the need to first move the data to a data lake or warehouse.

Domain-specific teams that manage, maintain, and provide data as a product are given ownership of the data by Data Mesh through the use of a decentralized model.

The primary objective of data mesh is to address the issues of data accessibility and availability at scale. Without the need of specialized data teams, business users and data scientists may access, analyze, and apply business insights from almost any data source, wherever.

In other words, data mesh improves data accessibility, discoverability, security, and interoperability. Faster access to query data directly translates into a faster time to value without the requirement for data transit.

Data Mesh requires a fundamental change in our assumptions, design, technology solutions, and social structure of our enterprises in order to manage, use, and own analytical data.

The data strategy is pushed away from analytical visualization and toward AI and real-time solutions. By adopting standards, definitions, and protocols that are particular to each choice and step of the procedure, data mesh addresses the basis of interoperability.

Chapter 1: Data Products

How Do Data Products Operate and What Are They?

Data products are developed with the idea that they will be used for a certain purpose. A data product can take on a variety of shapes depending on the particular business area or use case that must be addressed.

A data product is frequently linked to a corporate entity, such as a customer, asset, supplier, order, credit card, campaign, etc., that data consumers wish to access for analytical and operational purposes.

The product's data will most certainly be scattered over hundreds of siloed source systems, many of which will use various technologies, structures, formats, and terminologies. A data product therefore includes everything a data user needs to get value out of a business entity's data.

This includes the following characteristics of the good:

- Metadata that is both passive and active (usage and performance)
- Processing algorithms for the raw data that has been consumed
- Data post-processing (i.e., unified, cleansed, masked, enriched, etc.)
- Access techniques including streaming, CDC, JDBC, SQL, and others
- Synchronization regulations, which outline the manner and timing of data synchronization with source systems.
- Orchestrated data flows, as shown in a contemporary data catalog
- Systems of sources
- Data audit log changes
- Access controls such as authentication and credential checking

The data product delivery lifecycle adheres to the agile principles of being brief and iterative in order to provide immediate, incremental value to data users.

This is what a data product strategy entails:

1. Conceptualization

Data product requirements are determined using business objectives, data privacy and governance limitations, and existing data asset inventories. How data will be organized and componentized as a product for use with services will affect how a data product is designed.

2. Engineering

Locating, combining, and compiling data from many sources, then concealing it if necessary, are the steps involved in creating data products. Pipelines are secured to distribute the data to its constituents, and web service APIs are developed to allow access to the data product to consuming applications.

3. A guarantee of superior quality

The data is assessed and validated to ensure that it can be safely ingested by applications on a broad scale and that it is complete, compliant, and up to date.

4. Upkeep and assistance

In order to address problems as they develop, local authorities and data engineers regularly monitor data usage, pipeline performance, and reliability.

5. Management

Similar to a software product manager, a data product manager must identify and prioritize user needs before collaborating with the development and QA teams to ensure delivery. The data product manager is in responsible of delivering business value and ROI, where measurable targets have actual deadlines based on SLAs agreed upon between business and IT, such as reaction times for operational insights or the rate of application development.

Mesh

Innovative data product practices combine Design Thinking, which dismantles organizational barriers that inhibit cross-functional innovation, with the Jobs to Be Done Theory, which identifies the product's ultimate goal in accomplishing certain data customer goals.

Due to the quick uptake of cloud-based apps, distributed, microservices architectures are replacing centralized IT in application design (or a service mesh). The same pattern may be found in data architecture, when data is dispersed throughout numerous physical sites and facilities (or a data mesh).

Although a monolithic, centralized data architecture is typically simpler to develop and maintain, a modular, decentralized data management system has several compelling advantages in an IT environment that is quickly moving to the cloud.

Mesh's meaning

Technically speaking, a mesh is a network topology in which a group of non-hierarchical nodes interact together. Mesh is present in several locations, including:

- **Wifi Mesh:** WiFi mesh is the term for the situation where routers and extenders cooperate to expand Internet access.
- **5G Mesh:** A network of wireless clients, routers, and gateways known as 5G mesh is responsible for ensuring dependable cell phone connectivity.
- **Service Mesh:** Service Mesh is a single method for managing distributed microservices.

In place of the aforementioned, data mesh is a decentralized technique of sending data over large distances over physical and virtual networks. When compared to previous data integration solutions, a data mesh can function in on-premises, single-cloud, multi-cloud, and edge environments while still integrating data.

The Outcomes

In intricate and sizable organizations, data mesh sets are utilized to accomplish the following goals:

1. Adapt to change with grace because of a business's innate complexity, volatility, and uncertainty
2. Continue to be agile in the face of growth
3. Boost the data value to investment ratio.

These Changes

The multidimensional technical and organizational shifts introduced by Data Mesh depart from past analytical data management techniques.

Data mesh requires a fundamental change in our enterprises' underlying assumptions, designs, technical solutions, and social structures in terms of how we handle, use, and own analytical data:

Decentralized data ownership shifts away from centralized data ownership by experts who manage data platform technologies and toward a paradigm that gives ownership and accountability back to the business domains where data is generated or used.

In terms of architecture, it abandons the practice of storing data in rectangular warehouses and lakes and connects it instead through a dispersed mesh of data products that can be accessed through established protocols.

It goes away from technological solutions that view data as a result of pipeline code execution and moves in the direction of technological solutions that view data and code as a single, animate entity.

It changes the operational model of data governance from a top-down, centralized, human-intervened model to a federated model with computational policies encoded in the mesh's nodes.

Our value system is fundamentally altered from one in which we view data as an asset to be purchased to one in which we view it as a service to data users (internal and external to the organization).

It replaces two different sets of point-to-point, fragmented infrastructure services, one for data and analytics and the other for applications and operational systems, with a single, tightly integrated infrastructure that supports both operational and data systems.

Chapter 2: Principles of Data Mesh

Data mesh can be utilized as a component of an enterprise data strategy, expressing the intended state of the organizational operational model and the enterprise architecture through an iterative execution approach.

It can be expressed in terms of four interrelated principles in its most fundamental form.

Four straightforward concepts can be used to describe the logical architecture and operating paradigm of data mesh. These recommendations are meant to aid us in achieving the objectives of data mesh, which include maximizing the value of data at scale, preserving agility as an organization expands, and embracing change in a challenging and dynamic business environment.

Here's a quick summary of the guiding ideas.

1. **Data as a Product Principle**

   Domain-oriented data is delivered as a product directly with data users—data analysts, data scientists, and so on—with this paradigm in place.

A data product is a bundle of data sharing contracts that are clearly stated and simple to use. Each data product has its own life cycle and model, which is controlled independently of the others.

Data as a product provides a new logical architecture unit called data quantum, which controls and encapsulates all of the structural components required to exchange data as a product—data, metadata, code, policy, and infrastructure dependencies declarations— independently.

Data as a product follows a set of usability guidelines:

- Discoverable
- Addressable
- Understandable
- Dependable and truthful

- Natively available
- Composable and interoperable
- It is valuable in and of itself.
- Secure

Data as a product is motivated by the following goals:

- Changes the link between teams and data to eliminate the risk of domain-oriented data silos. Rather than collecting and siloing data, it becomes a product that teams share.

- Create a data-driven innovation culture by making the process of finding and using high-quality data peer-to-peer as frictionless as possible.

- Build change resilience into your data products with built-in and run-time isolation, as well as explicitly stated data sharing contracts, so that modifying one doesn't destabilize the others.

- By sharing and leveraging data across corporate boundaries, you may get more value out of it.

2. Domain Ownership Principle

This is the decentralization of ownership of analytical data to the business domains closest to it—either the data's source or its primary customers. Decompose (analytical) data logically and according to the business domain it represents, and manage the domain-oriented data life cycle independently.

Also it aligns business, technology, and analytical data architecturally and organizationally.

Domain ownership is motivated by the following factors:

- ❖ The ability to scale out data sharing corresponded to the axis of organizational growth: more data sources, more data consumers, and a greater variety of data use cases.

❖ By localizing change to business domains, optimization for continuous change can be achieved.

❖ Increasing agility by minimizing centralized bottlenecks in data teams, warehouses, and lake architecture and reducing cross-team synchronizations.

❖ Closing the gap between the data's true origin and where and when it's used for analytical use cases would improve data business truthfulness.

❖ By reducing cumbersome intermediary data pipelines, analytics and machine learning systems become more resilient.

3. The Self-Serve Data Platform principle

This idea has resulted in a new generation of self-serve data platform services that enable cross-functional domain teams to share data. The platform services are focused on removing friction from the data sharing path from source to consumption.

Individual data products are managed by platform services during their entire life cycle. They're in charge of a secure network of linked data items. They offer mesh-level interactions, such as displaying the emergent knowledge graph and lineage throughout the mesh.

The platform makes finding, accessing, and using data products easier for data users. It makes building, deploying, and maintaining data products easier for data suppliers.

The self-serve data platform is motivated by the following goals:

- Lower the entire cost of data decentralization.
- Domain teams' cognitive load in managing the end-to-end life cycle of their data products will be reduced by abstracting data management complexity.
- Reduce the need for specialization by mobilizing a bigger group of developers—technology generalists—to work on data product development.
- Create security and compliance standards for all data products with the use of automated governance policies.

4. Federated Computational Governance principle

Federated Computational Governance is a principle that governs how computers are used to make decisions.

This principle establishes a data governance operational model based on a federated decision-making and accountability structure, with a team of domain representatives, data platform specialists, and subject matter experts (legal, compliance, security, and so on).

The operational model establishes an incentive and accountability system that strikes a balance between domain autonomy and agility and mesh global interoperability. The governance execution model mainly relies on platform services to codify and automate regulations at a fine-grained level for each data product.

The following are the motivations for federated computational governance:

- The ability to extract higher-order value from the aggregation and correlation of disparate yet interoperable data sets.

- Domain incompatibility and disconnection are two negative implications of domain-oriented decentralization.

- Enabling cross-cutting governance requirements such as security, privacy, and legal compliance to be built into a mesh of distributed data products

- Manual synchronization between domains and the governance function is being reduced.

Chapter 3: Capabilities of Data Mesh

The following functional capabilities are supported by Data Mesh:

o **Catalog of data**

Data assets are discovered, classified, and inventoried, and information supply chains are clearly displayed.

o **Engineering with data**

Rapidly build scalable and dependable data pipelines for analytical and operational workloads. Domains can reuse common data preparation flows by productizing them.

o **Data management**

While preserving centralized control over company-wide data rules, distributes certain quality assurance, privacy compliance, and data availability policies and enforcement to business domains.

o **Organizing and preparing data**

Allows for fast orchestration of data flows from source to target, including data cleansing, transformation, masking, validation, and enrichment.

o **Integration and dissemination of data**

Data can be accessed from any source and piped to any target using any method: ETL (bulk), communications, CDC, virtualization, and APIs are all examples of ETL. Layer of data persistence

To improve data access performance, data is selectively stored and/or cached in the hub or within domains.

Non-functional capabilities are also addressed by data mesh:

- **Scale, volume, and performance of data**

Regardless of data amount, it scales up and down dynamically, flawlessly, and quickly.

- **Accessibility**

Supports all data source types, access modes, formats, and technologies, and integrates master and transactional data in both static and dynamic environments.

- **Distribution**

With perfect transactional integrity, it may be deployed on-premise, in the cloud, or in a hybrid environment.

- **Security**

To comply with privacy requirements, security encrypts and conceals data, and checks user credentials to ensure allowed access is maintained.

Use Cases for Data Mesh

Across multiple domains, Data Mesh supports a wide range of operational and analytical use cases. Listed below are a few examples:

- Customer 360-degree view: to assist customer service in reducing average handle time, improving first-contact resolution, and increasing customer satisfaction. Marketing can use a single view of the customer for predictive churn modeling or next-best-offer decisioning.

- Marketing teams can use hyper segmentation to send the appropriate campaign to the right customer at the right time and through the right channel.

- Data privacy management in the business areas to secure customer data by adhering with ever-emerging regional data privacy legislation, such as the VCDPA, before making it available to data consumers.

- Monitoring IoT devices gives product teams insights into edge device usage patterns, allowing them to improve product adoption and profitability over time.

- Domains can easily provision quality, trusted data for their data analytics workloads thanks to federated data preparation.

Factors that shape the application of data mesh

The application of data mesh to develop from viewing the world to affecting the world through data-driven value is shaped by five factors.

1. **Project Management**

Portfolio management is critical for maintaining order and guaranteeing alignment, speed, and reuse of capabilities when data products are defined at a more granular level.

Harmonizing data development with the larger solution and business digital portfolio gives data product portfolio management more power. As a result, data is aligned based on capacity, priority, and stated value and objectives.

2. **Semantics**

To describe and understand semantic perspectives, data mesh expands logical domain definitions and models. Working with data becomes declarative when business language is used in the form of relationships, classifications, labels, and tags.

Semantics enhances and speeds up the mapping between the proper data and what is needed in a business process in no-code/low-code application development settings. This means improved data and application interoperability.

3. Data Products

Services and APIs are used by applications to access data sources and pipelines. Data products are these parts or components.

A data source, event, query, schema, control, or insight is produced by a data product. They're built to meet the application's data requirements and handle the hard lifting of handling sophisticated data logic to make application process routing easier.

They also provide services to balance and optimize the cost-to-performance ratio for production payloads.

4. DataOps

DataOps is responsible for the quick and continual integration and deployment of data products, instead of data engineering and development for monolithic deployments.

At the enterprise and line of business levels, architects propose patterns and blueprints as beginning points for avoiding technological debt.

Data engineers own the products they create, which means DataOps is responsible for data provisioning quality, speed, and outcomes, as well as ongoing optimisation and life cycle management. As a result, data is guided by design rather than being an afterthought.

Chapter 4: Challenges of Data Mesh

The difficulty of managing different data products (and their connections) across multiple independent domains are the primary issues of a data mesh.

The following are the most important considerations:

1. Data duplication across domains

Redundancy, which occurs when data from one domain is repurposed to meet the demands of a different domain, can have an influence on resource utilization and data management expenses.

2. Data governance and quality assurance on a federated basis

When data products and pipelines are common commodities, different domains have different governance and quality criteria, which must be considered. Deltas must be recognized and federated as a result of this process.

3. Change management

To adopt a data mesh strategy, decentralizing data management necessitates significant change management in highly centralized data management techniques.

4. Risks and Costs

To enable a data mesh design, existing data and analytics technologies should be changed and enhanced. Setting up a data management infrastructure to support a data mesh, which includes data integration, virtualization, preparation, masking, governance, orchestration, cataloging, and distribution, may be a huge, expensive, and hazardous project.

5. Analytics that span multiple domains

To integrate the numerous data products and make them available to authorized users in one central location, an enterprise-wide data model must be created.

Benefits of Data Mesh

1. Business Agility and Scalability

Data mesh enables decentralized data operations, autonomous team performance, and data infrastructure as a service, resulting in faster time-to-market, scalability, and domain adaptability. It reduces operational and storage expenses by eliminating process complexities and IT backlog.

2. Data Security and Platform Connectivity

The decentralized architecture enables cloud apps to access to sensitive data stored on-site, which may be streamed live or stored on devices in real time. Instead of asking users to create a copy and route it across a public network to a data warehouse, Data Mesh queries/compiles data analytics where the data sits.

Through platform connection in a distributed model, it minimizes the danger of data breach or information loss to increase security and decreases data latency to improve overall performance in many use cases such as live streaming, online gaming, financial trading, and so on.

3. Flexibility and autonomy

Enterprises that use data mesh architecture become vendor neutral, meaning they aren't tied to a single data platform. Due to connectors to a variety of systems, the distributed infrastructure provides businesses with unrivaled flexibility and options.

4. Get More Out of Distributed Data with Data Mesh in Action

For organizations, data mesh opens up a world of possibilities in a variety of consumption situations, including behavior modeling, analytics, and data-intensive applications. It might be core data, such as sales data, or non-core data, such as web data and clickstream; the distributed design allows for easier data access and quicker delivery without the need for an expensive corporate warehouse or vendor lock-in.

5. Improved Transparency Through Multi-Functional Teams

Traditional data platforms' centralized data ownership isolates expert teams, lacks transparency, and fails to provide a backup plan in the event that data control/ownership is lost. Through its domain-oriented approach, Data Mesh decentralizes data ownership by distributing it among cross-functional domain teams, such as domain experts, business teams, IT, and agile virtual teams, for improved transparency and data quality.

6. Access to information more quickly and with greater accuracy

Data mesh provides a consolidated and easily manageable infrastructure based on a self-service paradigm that eliminates underlying complexity, allowing for quicker data access and correct delivery.

With SQL queries, businesses may access data from anywhere at a significantly lower latency. The distributed design cuts down on the processing and intervention levels, which slow down the time it takes to get insight.

7. End-to-end compliance requires robust data governance

Data ingestion is reconciled with its sources, formats, and volumes using distributed architecture, allowing businesses to control security at the source system. Decentralized data operations make it easier to follow global data governance requirements for high-quality data delivery and data accessibility.

Chapter 5: How to build a data mesh

It would be both lengthy and complicated to describe how to build and implement a data mesh in detail. However, there are three main stages to consider in the process.

1. Addressable

Make all of your relevant data addressable so it can be easily found. Use the RESTful approach and make all of your bucket names consistent. This can help you standardize all of your data and make it more accessible. Then consider adding service level agreements (SLAs) to all end points and monitoring those endpoints to ensure data is always available.

After that, re-route any query engines and BI tools you're using so they can access and use these new data products. If you're working with data warehouses or lakes, take the same approach and create standardized schemas and views for them as well. This phase will be carried out in a centralized manner by your data platform teams.

2. Catalogue

Boost the quality of your metadata and data catalogs. As a result, your data will be more discoverable, allowing anybody inside your business to access and consume data products. You'll need a 'site' where people can search for, find, and access the information they require. You'll also need to set up a system that allows both data owners and consumers to seek and get access to your data products without the need for a central team.

You should also consider adding tests that measure the data's quality, as well as lineage and monitoring, at this point. These tests should be applied to both moving and static data. You might want to think about where a CI testing process fits in at this point.

3. DDD

Break or move away from past monolithic data structures by implementing DDD. This is a significant step toward the creation of a decentralized architecture.

One way to do this is to assign ownership to the domain team that is producing the data.

Your teams must be responsible for their own data assets, quality testing and monitoring, ETL pipelines, testing, and other factors. It's also important to keep in mind that federated governance is required to ensure security, interoperability, and data standardization.

When all of this is in place, it reduces the need for changes, especially major ones. All you have to do now is make sure these features are available as services so you can build your self-service platform. This is also the stage at which you'll introduce your DataOps practices and work on improving self-service and observational capabilities.

Using a Data Product Platform to Implement Data Mesh

A real-time data product platform, based on a decentralized design pattern, is the best implementation for data mesh architecture.

A data product platform develops and delivers data products made up of connected data from many sources to give operational and analytical workloads a real-time and holistic perspective of the business.

The semantic definition of the numerous data products that are crucial to the business is created via a real-time data product platform. It also establishes the data intake procedures and central governance policies required to protect and secure data in data products in line with regulations.

Additional platform nodes are deployed in accordance with the business domains, allowing the domains to oversee and govern data services and pipelines for their particular data consumers.

1. **Budget:** Let's start with the hypothetical deal breaker: Will the domains be able to afford to build their infrastructure, develop applications, offer data products, and maintain them? Even if the calculations appear to be correct, there are

other dangers to be aware of. Assume that the Platform Team has created a tool that effectively bridges the technological divide.

However, as time goes on, volumes get larger, data products become more complicated (as with any other IT project), and they may find themselves having to pay far more than they can afford.

2. **Taking on a Certain Amount of Work:** Keeping in mind that your domain teams are also undergoing significant change, the Platform Team will need to put in far more effort than usual. Even if the domains are internal customers, the way they deliver has some criteria. Any migration that produces breaking changes after the domains have been onboarded might be a headache. As a result, your Platform Team will have 10% of the flexibility it had while designing a typical data platform right from the start.

3. **Very Strong Central/Organizational Owner:** We've said it before and we'll say it again: Data Mesh deployment is more about organizational change than technological transformation. It will take a lot of organizational support because it pushes a lot of changes that some people are afraid of. It's easy to fail without a strategy, an acknowledged action plan, and a greater awareness of what we're trying to accomplish within the organization.

4. **Convince Domains to Cooperate:** Because Data Mesh adds a lot of extra work for domains (they used to just consume reports), you'll need to persuade them that it's worth it. You must continue coordinate important releases with them once they are on board. Assume you want to update the platform, which will result in some breaking changes, but one domain is now testing new applications. They have the ability to put you off for months. It could be worthwhile to

create a release calendar or a guide for platform-domain team collaboration, RACI, and so on.

Are you prepared to set up a data mesh?

You've probably realized the benefits of data meshing and that it's not a passing fad. You may even believe it is something that you should consider implementing, but where do you begin? The first thing to keep in mind is that data mesh is still a relatively new concept, so make ensure that you are prepared to adopt and adapt it.

The second point to keep in mind is that there is no single type of data mesh; rather, there are a variety of them. Some are primarily centralized, while others are predominantly decentralized. It is not only difficult, but also time-consuming to migrate to the latter type. Many of your challenges will be technical, but the most important one will be changing your organizational mindset.

Companies that were founded on a hierarchical and centralized model have organizational attitudes. This creates a significant hurdle to transitioning away from existing approaches, which is why relatively few companies have used decentralized microservices. So, how can you tell if your company is ready for data mesh?

1. Establish a framework

The structure of your company should be based on business domains or comprised of cross-functional teams. If your product, engineering, and QA teams are all working in silos, you'll need to get them to collaborate before implementing data mesh.

2. Focus

You need a strong DevOps focus, with all members of your team looking to build automated services, ideally with a GitOps angle.

3. Platform

You should be using a modern platform that allows for high productivity while keeping technical details hidden from users. A self-service infrastructure also necessitates a certain level of abstraction. A service mesh can also be used to connect the various networking aspects of your architecture.

4. Streaming

You'll need a streaming engine platform to move forward. You can't migrate to microservices and unify batch and streaming without such a platform. It also aids in the reconciliation of OLTP (online transaction processing) and OLAP (online analytical processing) workloads. These platforms can be used to create event-driven microservices or to move data.

5. Migration

Make the switch to microservices. This is a significant step that necessitates understanding how DDD (domain driven design) works. When you understand DDD and how to split your microservices into different business domains, it'll be much easier to do the same with your data products.

6. Big data

You will find implementing data mesh difficult or unnecessary if you are unfamiliar with big data, how it works, and what its implications are.

7. Metadata

Learn how to address, discover, and catalog your data, as well as how to manage metadata.

The tale isn't over with the data mesh yet

Now that we've shown that the data mesh needs a data foundation to work properly, let's take a look at where it leads. If your objective is to create value from the data, how do you realize the results of your data mesh? In this case, data products are useful.

We are all aware that how data is used determines its worth. I'm not referring to straightforward dashboards. I'm referring to sophisticated and comprehensive data solutions that urge you to act in order to add value and protect your customers, employees, and business. Think of fraud prediction for your bank accounts, anomaly detection for your networks, or real-time recommendation engines that enhance customer experiences.

In other words, the data ocean is the architectural foundation and the data mesh is the organizational model that enable your team to develop data products. If every corporation is a "data company," then its currency is the "data goods" it can provide, together with their repeatability and reliability.

Conclusion

Data mesh is incredibly helpful for businesses and society at large. It changes the emphasis from analytical to more realistic approaches.

This book does this topic justice by outlining everything you need to know about data mesh. In the end, if the Data Mesh principles are wisely applied, society will gain much.